HAPP' MEMORIAL Day

USA

4th july

COLORING BOOK FOR ADULTS

Happy Memorial Day!

We
Honor
You.
Thank you.

MEMORIAL DAY

☆ USA ☆

MEMORIAL
DAY

REMEMBER
OUR
HEROES

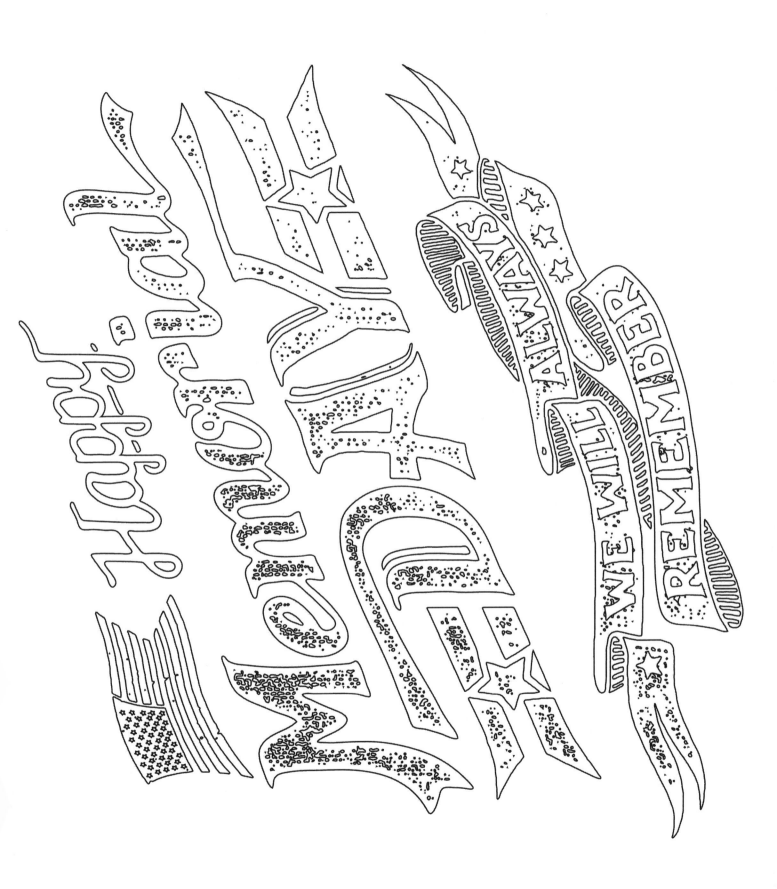

Join Us >> bit.ly/get_sample_free

- Get Free "Reviw Copies" of our New releases
- Exclusive offers and book giveaways
- More events from our community

Thank you